My Beautiful Country

Fabiola Sepulveda

Notes for the Grown-ups

This wordless book allows for a rich shared reading experience for children who do not yet know how to read or who are beginning to learn. Children can look at the pages to gather information from what they see, and they can suggest text to tell the story they want to tell.

To extend this reading experience, do one or more of the following:

Discuss what makes a place beautiful.

Introduce vocabulary such as these words when looking at the pictures and telling the story you see:

- beach
- canyon
- cave
- earth
- grass
- land
- mountain
- ocean
- river
- rocks
- sand
- sky
- water
- waterfall
- valley

Ask the child what they might do at each of these settings. Have they visited any of these places before or places like them?

After reading the pictures, come back to the book again and again. Rereading is an excellent tool for building literacy skills.

Talk about the images and what you see. Find a list of locations on page 24.

Consultant

Cynthia Malo, M.A.Ed.

Publishing Credits

Rachelle Cracchiolo, M.S.Ed., *Publisher*
Emily R. Smith, M.A.Ed., *SVP of Content Development*
Véronique Bos, *VP of Creative*
Dona Herweck Rice, *Senior Content Manager*

Image Credits: all images from iStock and/or Shutterstock

Library of Congress Cataloging in Publication Control Number:
2024013627

p. 2 Rainbow Falls, Hawaii
p. 3 Oahu, Hawaii
pp. 4–5 Glacier Bay National Park, Alaska
p. 6 Yosemite National Park, California
p. 7 Horseshoe Bend, Arizona
pp. 8–9 Yellowstone National Park, Wyoming
p. 10 Zion National Park, Arizona
p. 11 Durango, Colorado
p. 12 Duluth, Minnesota
p. 13 Lake Michigan, Illinois
p. 14 New York City, New York
p. 15 Myrtle Beach, South Carolina
pp. 16–17 Everglades, Florida
pp. 18–19 San Juan, Puerto Rico
pp. 20–21 Niagra Falls, New York

TCM Teacher Created Materials

5482 Argosy Avenue
Huntington Beach, CA 92649
www.tcmpub.com
ISBN 979-8-7659-6136-0
© 2025 Teacher Created Materials, Inc.
Printed by: 926. Printed in: Malaysia. PO#: PO11723